MW01222635

Great ac
of reader. Through the River and Fire is an exciting and gripping account of the author's experience in the harsh conditions in the Arctic and a memorable testimonial to the devastating power of fire

Laurel Lowry
IT Consultant and mother of four.

Steve Gallant's recounting of this dangerous military mission is a testimony to the skill and training of the Canadian military. A must read for boys and girls with a love of adventure

Ken Jones
Teacher

This page turner pulls you along through adventures jam packed with obstacles and dangers. Join Lieutenant Gallant and his men on their mission as they face their fears, conquer overwhelming obstacles, and work together as they face the challenges of the cruel North

Terry Loerts
BA, MEd.

Advance to Adventure

R. Stephen Gallant

Advance to Adventure

vol I: Through the River and Fire

TATE PUBLISHING & Enterprises

Published by Tate Publishing & Enterprises, LLC
127 E. Trade Center Terrace | Mustang, Oklahoma 73064 USA
1.888.361.9473 | www.tatepublishing.com

Tate Publishing is committed to excellence in the publishing industry. The company reflects the philosophy established by the founders, based on Psalm 68:11,
"The Lord gave the word and great was the company of those who published it."

Book design copyright © 2008 by Tate Publishing, LLC. All rights reserved.
Cover design by Nathan Harmony
Interior design by Jacob Crissup
Illustrations by Brandon Wood

Published in the United States of America

ISBN: 978-1-60462-738-1
1. Juvenile Nonfiction: Adventure & Adventurers/People & Places: Canadian Arctic
2. Youth & Children: Christian Non-Fiction: Adventure
08.03.04

Dedication

To my wonderful wife, Marina,
thank you for everything.

Acknowledgements

Firstly I acknowledge Jesus, my personal Lord and Saviour, in all of my ways. Without His amazing grace numerous times throughout my life, I would not be alive today.

In addition, this book would not have been possible without the continued love and support of my wife Marina. I owe a debt of gratitude to my kids who insisted constantly that I "tell them another story." Their persistence lead to the idea to write a non-fiction book for young readers full of adventure and demonstration of God's miraculous saving power.

Table of Contents

Foreword

Mission impossible? It certainly seemed that way for Lieutenant Stephen Gallant, platoon commander of thirty-two of Canada's best, stranded on an insignificant ledge next to a raging, ice-cold river. In his own words: "No one conquers the Arctic. The best one can hope for is to survive its lessons and to achieve your goal."

When you read the pages of *Through the River and Fire* you move quickly from spectator to participant—you feel as if you are a member of the platoon! Who needs video games when you can train alongside Gallant's men at CFB Petawawa.

Rumble through the sky in a C130 Hercules aircraft. Fill your lungs with fresh Arctic air. Hunker down in a 15-man assault boat and hit the rapids of unforgiving Arctic waterways. These are but a few adventures that await you when you volunteer to follow Lieutenant Gallant on his 550 kilometer trek across some of the most rugged terrain the military has ever tackled. If the river wasn't tough enough, follow Gallant through the *fire* in Part Two of this exciting book! I believe we serve a God of rescue. Whether it's saving people from sin or alerting them to imminent physical danger, Jesus saves!

In one sense this book is a testament to the importance of planning, teamwork, sacrifice, leadership and perseverance—values and characteristics we should all strive to possess. In another sense, it is a personal testimony about a loving God who is eager to get involved in *all* of our lives. Yes, I said *all!* Whether you feel on top of the world or you've never felt lower, *Through the River and Fire* reminds us that we cannot do it on our own. Just when you think you haven't got a prayer. You do. And He will answer.

"This poor man called, and the Lord heard him; he saved him out of all his troubles" (Psalm 34:6).

"I began to think that my men just followed me to find out what would happen next," mused the Lieutenant.

Want to find out what happens next? Okay then, let's go...

Brad Sumner
Youth Pastor
Ontario, Canada

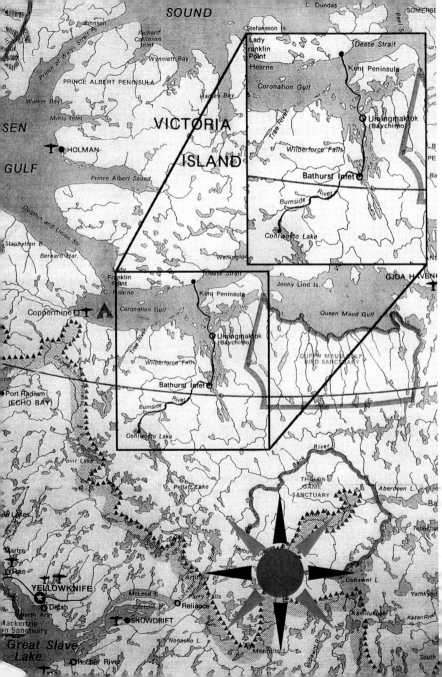

Part 1
Through the River

The Beginning

As I stood, bathing in a frigid pool of Arctic water on an endless plain of tundra in the Northwest Territories, I was reminded that man is an incredibly insignificant being. The overwhelming feelings at that moment were ones of fear, loneliness, and excitement. I had to continually look back to our small camp in the distance to reassure myself that I was not the last person on the planet. Thirty-two other small forms moved about our camp. They were my men, I was their leader, and we had come to challenge the Canadian Arctic.

The Canadian Arctic is one of the last frontiers

left in the world. It's a land of incomprehensible vastness and beauty—a harsh unforgiving land, filled with dangers, where the weak perish and the strong grow. No one conquers the Arctic. The best one can hope for is to survive its lessons and to achieve your goal.

Where should I start? Oh, I guess the beginning would be nice. I have a passion for the Arctic.

It was 1985. The planning for this Arctic military expedition began more than 1,500 miles to the south and several months before hand. I became involved when I volunteered and was selected to lead the expedition. My mission was to lead a platoon of militia and regular force soldiers on a 550 kilometer trip. We would travel by fifteen- man assault boats (large rubber boats/rafts) from Contwoyto Lake to Victoria Island, Northwest Territories. Our route would go from the Lupin Mine site on Contwoyto Lake into Kathawachage Lake, along the Burnside River into Bathurst Inlet, up Bathurst Inlet, and across to Byron Bay, Victoria Island. We were to spend eighteen days training, and thirty-three days in the Arctic itself. This type of exercise had never before been attempted by the military.

I was selected as platoon commander, while a regular force Captain by the name of Pat Henneberry was to handle logistical arrangements and to act as "safety officer." Command of the troops and the accomplishment of the mission rested squarely on my shoulders. Captain Henneberry was to intervene only if safety became a factor.

Time was critical. Long and frantic hours were spent making a million and one arrangements. There were not enough hours in the day. Captain Henneberry and I both decided that a trip to Yellowknife to coordinate the support we required from the Northern Regional Headquarters was essential. Besides, I had never been to Yellowknife before.

Yellowknife

Yellowknife is a great place. The town is not very big, only about ten thousand people. It was (and still is) a gold mining town. Government is the largest employer. In the summer there is a tremendous boom in population. Exploration companies looking for oil, gold, and other metals fly in workers. The construction firms add more workers. All building is done in the summer months because of the harsh conditions of the winter. The rapid growth of Yellowknife has made it a place with a critical housing shortage. You do not go to work in Yellowknife, or anywhere else in the Arctic, without having prearranged your accommodation. Yellowknife, the regional capital of the Northwest Territories, has a reasonably good airport. The place is the gateway between other parts of the Arctic and the south, and a lot of transient people visit the town.

Summer is also the main tourist season. Thousands of eager people, from the world over, arrive to explore the Arctic's wonders. The abundant wildlife (by southern standards), great fishing, and exciting landscapes are just some of the attractions. Yellowknife also does reasonably well in the winter with Japanese tours flying in and bussing out to stand on the frozen Great Slave Lake to watch the Northern Lights.

Yellowknife is still a frontier town. The air is clean and crisp. There is an excitement and energy in the atmosphere that is hard to describe. I love it.

Henneberry and I stood outside at twelve midnight with the sun still in the sky. We were in the "land of the midnight sun." Neither of us wanted to go to bed. The streets were still packed with people. We reluctantly returned to our rooms, but I slept only a little. I was too excited.

The next morning we walked to the Canadian

Forces Northern Region Headquarters (NRHQ). We met the staff and spent the morning discussing our expedition and Northern Command's role in it. Captain John Todd was to meet us at Bathurst Inlet to assist us in our travel up the Inlet and across to Victoria Island. Other assistance would be provided by NRHQ's two Twin Otter aircraft (one float and one wheeled) to preposition supplies at certain points along our route.

NRHQ had large maps of the region, which they agreed to give us. We discussed danger areas along our route. We needed outboard engines to get us across the two lakes in the time allotted (35-horsepower minimum given the size of the loads in the boats). The Burnside River had a large number of rapids that would have to be reconnoitered and possibly portaged around, depending on the water level. At the end of the Burnside River at Bathurst Inlet was the Burnside Falls. The portage around the falls was four miles over rugged terrain. I was not looking forward to this part of the trip since we would be carrying massive loads. Bathurst Inlet is part of the Arctic Ocean and we would have to carry all of our drinking water with us from then on. More weight. We planned to island hop up the Inlet in case we ran into a storm. The most dangerous portion of the trip would be the crossing of the forty miles of open ocean from the Kent Peninsula to Victoria Island in rubber boats. If we got caught in bad weather, we were finished. A capsized boat in Arctic waters means that the occupants have a few minutes to live before they are overcome with hypothermia. The water temperature ranges between zero to 3 degrees Celsius (or 32 to 40 degrees Fahrenheit). If we got stranded somewhere in the Inlet, NRHQ would have a difficult time mounting a rescue with only two Twin Otters and very few suitable landing areas. Overall, I got the impression that the staff at NRHQ thought we were crazy. They probably were right, but I didn't think up the expedition, I was only given the job of doing it.

The afternoon was spent going over countless details about the expedition. The next day we left Yellowknife to begin eighteen days of training at Canadian Forces Base, Petawawa.

Petawawa: Training and Preparation

The training was physically and mentally demanding. We tried to weed out unsuitable candidates for the expedition. Forty-four candidates had volunteered, and by the end of eighteen days, we were down to twenty-nine.

Training involved a number of subjects such as northern climate, geography, history, and people, as well as map work, navigation, communications, small engine operation and repair, and northern survival. Normal compasses are next to useless in the Arctic because of the close proximity to the magnetic North Pole. We trained on a special compass called the Astro Compass, which utilizes the sun's position to determine direction. Communication is also a problem in the Arctic because of the vast distances involved. The military's answer to long distance communication was the 515 set, which is a heavy (about twenty-five pounds) and expensive radio (about $18,000). We trained on its set-up and operation, and we tested these wonderful radios in Petawawa, too bad they never worked in the Arctic.

Extensive training was completed on the fifteen-man assault boat. Loading, unloading, maintenance, and handling were all covered. Then into the water for a lot of work with white water techniques. We learned to read rivers and rapids, select routes, and maneuver our boats through white water. The rapids on the Ottawa, Petawawa, and Matawa rivers served as our training area.

Medical and dental check-ups were done on all personnel. There would be no hospitals close by to assist us. We had to be fit prior to departure, and we reviewed first aid at length for the trip. We had to be self-sufficient and be able to handle any emergency. A very highly- qualified regular force medic was assigned to the expedition. He brought a supply of drugs with him and could deal with any medical situation up to and including minor surgery.

Another major test was the swim test. Most of our time was going to be spent on water and having a non-swimmer in the group could jeopardize lives. We conducted the test at the Base's pool, but the catch was we did it fully clothed (we wouldn't be wearing bathing suits in the Arctic). Swimming lengths, treading water, and performing rescue techniques takes on a new meaning when you are weighed down with a full set of clothing. I didn't know it at the time, but this test would become a brutal reality in the Arctic.

Physical training was a daily occurrence. At 5:30 a.m. each morning, I would lead the men in stretching, push-ups, sit-ups, runs, and team sports. It was my favorite part of the day. I set the minimum acceptable chin-up standard of seven consecutive chin-ups (with arms fully extended). At the beginning, very few candidates could do any, let alone seven, but by the end of the training phase all could do the seven chin-ups. It was a tremendous sense of accomplishment for them.

Under my command were two regular force and twenty-nine reserve force personnel. The regular force persons were my second-in-command, Warrant Officer Doug Hilchey, and my medic, Sergeant Wayne Gibson. The platoon was divided up into three sections. My section commanders were Sergeant Quickfall (one section), Master-Corporal Kolmer (two section), and Sergeant Martin (three section). Captain Henneberry, as the safety officer, brought our total group to thirty-three.

On the 20th of July, we moved to Ottawa. Everyone got one day off and then we packed for the trip north. Packing for the trip sounds easy. It wasn't. We were moving to the Arctic, conducting an extensive expedition, and had to be totally self-sufficient for thirty-three days. To get an idea of the scope of the equipment we took with us, let's look at some of it. The load included: seven 15-man assault boats (over two hundred pounds each); eight 35-horsepower outboard engines (one was a spare; over eighty pounds each); eight 45-gallon drums of gasoline and cans of oil for the engines; six 45-gallon drums of aviation fuel for the two Twin Otter aircraft (as mentioned before, they were used to preposition supplies along our route—we had to bring fuel for them with us because gas stations are in short supply in the Arctic); 280 cases of rations (close to 1000 pounds and a lot of bulk); four 10-man Arctic tents (about two hundred pounds), two 515-sets (our wonder radios); seven 25-sets (short range radio's, they at least worked); stoves and cooking equipment; thirty-one FNC1 rifles; one general purpose machine gun, ammunition (lots and lots of ammunition), and thirty-three rucksacks (containing personal kit and sleeping bags). This list is by no means exhaustive. It took two C130 Hercules aircraft (the work-horse transport aircraft of the Canadian Forces), fully loaded, to deliver us to the Lupin Mine site. We were required to portage four miles around the Burnside Falls carrying this gear. Any wonder why I stressed physical fitness during the training phase?

On the 23rd of July we walked on to the tarmac at Canadian Forces Base Ottawa to the waiting aircraft. The Arctic and its wonders lay ahead.

Contwoyto Lake: Arrival in the Arctic

I stepped off the plane at Lupin Mine site, Contwoyto Lake, Northwest Territories and fell in love. The air was clean and crisp. The terrain was barren plains of rugged tundra for as far as the eye could see in every direction. It filled me with a feeling of excitement and energy that didn't leave me for thirty-three days. This was wild beautiful country with breath taking scenery.

There were no trees since we were far above the tree line. The wind was a constant factor, and it only changed in degree of force. But the wind was a welcome friend because it kept down the bugs.

When ever we were in sheltered or in low-lying terrain, the bugs would come out in force. I'm not talking about the odd fly that disturbs your tranquil barbecue, but rather black swarms of bugs that would cover your clothes and fill every orifice. That's right, ears, nose, and mouth. If you didn't have a bug net over you head, you either spent a lot of time gagging on bugs or you kept your mouth shut.

Lupin Mine is a gold mine owned by Echo Bay Mines. We arranged with the mine manager for a fork lift and a large flatbed truck to unload and transport our equipment to our campsite by the lake. Without their assistance we would have spent unknown man hours in back-breaking labour.

We set up camp and spent a very busy week preparing for our expedition and acclimatizing. Captain Henneberry and I went on the Twin Otter aircraft to pre-position the supplies. The more we could pre-position along the seven drop-off points, the less we had to carry. I saw a lot of the area from the air. The boats were organized, packed, and checked out.

Early on we discovered the 515 radio sets were useless. They worked in Petawawa, but not in the

Arctic. Being good soldiers we were supposed to check in with Yellowknife the same time everyday, and we did. For thirty-three days, we would stop what we were doing at noon, climb to a high point, set up the 515 radio set, and try to contact Yellowknife. No one ever answered. It gave the men an opportunity to take a break each day. The problem was very serious. After we left Lupin Mine (where we had access to their radio) we would be totally out of contact with the world. If an emergency happened, we would have to survive on our own. Warrant Officer Hilchey arranged with a Bow Valley helicopter pilot (Bow Valley was another company doing exploration in the area) to fly over us while we were on the river portion of our expedition every two days or so. If we waved a red scarf then we had an emergency situation and he would land, otherwise we were okay. It cost us a couple of cases of rations (the helicopter pilot used them on fishing trips), but he was our only link with civilization.

We had brought weapons to the Arctic. Most of the weapons and ammunition were to be used for planned fire power demonstrations for the native people. This is a form of "military public relations."

You fire a bunch of weapons to demonstrate your prowess and then allow the locals to fire a few rounds (under strict supervision). The people loved it. One elderly Inuit man asked me if he could borrow our machine gun to go fishing. I wasn't sure how he was going to accomplish this, but I had to tell him that military regulations prevented us from loaning out our machine gun.

Captain Henneberry and I were carrying some special ammunition rounds for the greatest animal danger to man in the Arctic. We had 7.62 mm hollow point rounds for the polar bears. That cute, friendly-looking white bear in the Southern zoo is, in the Arctic, a fierce hunter who is not afraid of anything. If something moves in the Arctic, then it is prey for the polar bears. These magnificent powerful kings of the north can out run and out swim any man. The bottom line is, a polar bear decides you're his next meal, you either kill it or it kills you.

On the lighter side, we all threw a buck into the pot to see who could catch the biggest fish. When I say fishing, please read "essential survival skills," due to the need to supplement our daily rations. Anyone who has eaten military rations for a long period of time will support this necessity. Sergeant Gibson won the contest by catching an 18-pound trout. Not a large fish by Arctic standards, but respectable for Southern folk like us.

Sergeant Gibson had brought a crossbow to the Arctic with him. One day the men set up a target and were taking turns firing the weapon. A good shot was when someone hit the target. I made the mistake of walking by the group at the firing line.

"Hey, sir, why don't you take a turn?" One man offered.

"Yeah, you can show us how it's done," another said. Enlisted men the world over like to see officers embarrass themselves. I was handed the crossbow before I could think of a way out of the situation. "Go for it, sir," another soldier said.

I had never fired a crossbow before. I was what you would call an average shot with a rifle (I could generally hit the target), but a crossbow? Everyone was watching as I aimed the weapon. Line up the sites, get a site picture, breath out half way, hold the breath, squeeze the trigger slowly with even pressure, and oh yes, pray for a reasonable shot. Whoop! Off the arrow goes. Bulls-eye! Bulls-eye?

Yes, a perfect bulls-eye! The men were all standing around with their mouths hanging open. I handed the crossbow back, told them that I would fire it again when someone could beat my shot, and made a quick exit. I think I was in greater shock than any of my men. It was a once in a life time shot, which I could never duplicate (without years of practice). I never had to do it again because no one beat my shot. I retired the champion and had upheld the prowess of the officer corps.

The manager of the mine site gave us a tour of the mine (no gold samples), and fed us a meal of hamburgers and fries. But there was a catch. We were challenged to a game of baseball. The miners were very worried beforehand that the big tough military would beat them badly. They stacked their team against us by adjusting shifts so that their best players could play us. The game started and they stopped worrying about us when they had us by 30 to 0 after two innings. Who would have thought that I needed a baseball team in the middle of the Arctic?

Burnside River: Growth

It was time to leave the relative comfort of our camp site on Contwoyto Lake. All preparations had been made. Supplies pre-positioned, boats loaded, and men eager to get underway. The ice in the river had melted. The river and the mission were calling.

We departed early on the morning of the 30th of July. The temperature was cold, the wind biting and the rain continual. Captain Henneberry's boat's engine would not start. It had worked in all the trials, but failed when we needed it. Time was lost as we changed it for our only spare engine. We decided to carry the broken engine on the trip so that we could cannibalize it for spare parts if needed. We finally got underway with my boat leading and Captain Henneberry's in the rear. The rain and high winds slowed our progress on Contwoyto Lake. Being cold is one thing, but being wet and cold is far worse.

In between Contwoyto Lake and Kathawachage Lake there is a short stretch of river where we encountered our first set of rapids. I established an operating procedure for rapids where I would go forward on foot to reconnoiter the rapids and return to brief the other boat commanders on the best approach to shooting them. I tried to take different boat commanders with me to teach them what I was looking for and get their opinions. We would then set off, with my boat leading.

At the first set of rapids, Sergeant Quickfall's boat got hung up on some rocks and became stuck in the middle of the rapids. Captain Henneberry's boat came by the place in the river where I was waiting, and he advised me that he was going to see what was up ahead. The platoon waited for Quickfall's boat to get free. I was in radio contact with Quickfall and he assured me that he could get the boat off the rocks. Master Corporal Kolmer's boat was going to assist in the extraction. Henneberry had moved so far ahead, he was barely audible on the radio. Then a member of Kolmer's boat fell in the water trying to assist Quickfall's crew.

That was it. Time for action. I called Henneberry and advised him that I had a man in the water who required treatment for hypothermia. I then ordered Kolmer to wrap his man in an emergency blanket and proceed down the river to find Captain Henneberry who should have a camp set up with a stove going. Hypothermia was nothing to fool around with in these fridged conditions.

"Corporal Specht," I said to the man at the controls of my boat, "get me back up river to Quickfall's boat."

"Yes, sir," Specht replied and turned us up river.

"Corporal Marshal, dig out a rope. When we get to shore, you come with me, Sergeant Gibson and Corporal Specht can stay with the boat."

"What are you going to do?" asked Sergeant Gibson.

"I don't know. We have to get them off those rocks. I'll make it up when I get there."

It didn't take long. Specht dropped us near the base of the rapids and Marshal and I moved by foot to a point across from Quickfall's boat.

They were hung up good. All the other boats in the platoon were now down river and couldn't help. I had to get the rope to Quickfall, who was about sixty feet from shore. Several attempts at throwing one end of the rope were unsuccessful because of the distance. Options were limited. I took off my rain gear, sweater, shirt, and emptied my pockets. I then tied one end of the rope around my waist.

"Sir," Marshal said, "that water is moving very fast and it's freezing. There has got to be a better way."

"Can you think of one?" I asked.

"No," Marshal said. "But let me do it, sir."

"No, Marshal, I appreciate the offer but, it's my job. Just don't let go of your end of the rope." I said as I moved into the water. *Cold! Penetrating cold!* I kept moving. Up to my waist and then I slipped and went to my neck before I could recover my footing. That sucked in the breath.

"Quickfall!" I yelled over the noise of the river.

"Yes, sir," he replied.

"You better appreciate this," I said.

"Isn't it cold, sir?" Quickfall asked.

"Cold does not describe it!" Talking was helping me take my mind off of the situation. "How's it going, Corporal Todd?" Todd was in the front of Quickfall's boat. He kept smiling and shaking his head at me.

"Better than you're doing at the moment, sir," Todd replied. Todd was an honest guy.

Oh was it cold, I was at mid-chest level now, and I was going numb all over. "I'd appreciate it if you guys would put some effort into getting yourselves off the rocks!" They all started paddling and rocking their boat. Just before I got to them, they got off the rocks! I was standing in the middle of a set of rapids frozen stiff for nothing! They waved to me as they moved down river.

I turned around and made my way back to shore. Sergeant Gibson had an emergency blanket waiting for me at my boat. I called Henneberry on the radio. Kolmer had arrived at his location and his man who had fallen in the water earlier was okay.

"Great," I said over the radio. "Quickfall's boat

is now free of the rocks and moving towards your location. I'll have another hypothermia case to you shortly."

"Another case? Who is it?" Henneberry said.

"Me! Over and out!" I was upset. What a start to the trip!

Captain Henneberry and Warrant Officer Hilchey had set up the platoon campsite. It was only supposed to be an emergency one to render treatment to Kolmer's man, but it was late and getting dark so they decided to stop for the night. The problem was, they set up camp in a bug-infested bog.

I was the last boat in to the campsite. I stripped and got into a sleeping bag. Hot coffee helped. Hilchey told me that what I had done was very brave. Certainly not the brightest thing he had ever heard of, but brave none the less. Henneberry went on at length about exposing myself to unnecessary risks and danger. He said I was the platoon commander, and thus the platoon's most valuable member. I told him I only knew of one way to lead and that was from the front. The discussion ended.

We spent a miserable night in the bog swatting the swarms of insects, and trying to stay dry.

My air mattress was floating in water by morning. The bugs were vicious and morale was low. After a quick meal we moved off. I wanted to get away from the bog as quickly as possible.

Over the course of days, we crossed Kathawachage Lake and moved into the Burnside River. It was amazing, and the sun came out the moment we entered the river. Morale improved. We encountered several sets of rapids that were not serious, which helped improve our skill and confidence.

My boat had just taken a very long set of rapids and we were drifting in calm water waiting for the other boats to catch up. I was looking up river for our boats when suddenly Sergeant Gibson jumped to his feet in the boat.

"Why does the horizon disappear?" he asked urgently. I jumped up to join him.

"I don't know," I said, but the horizon did disappear not far in front of us. Our boat was picking up speed.

"It's a waterfall!" Gibson yelled.

"Specht, get the engine going and get us out of here!" I yelled.

"No time! We are going to go over it!" Gibson yelled. "Head for the opening to the left!"

We all grabbed our paddles and worked frantically. We rocketed through the opening between two rocks and sailed through the air. I never knew that fully loaded rubber boats could fly. I think we were all screaming. We hit the bottom and water poured over the front of the boat in a giant wave. Gibson and I, who were in the front of the boat, were soaked and almost knocked overboard.

Looking back, we saw a waterfall about ten feet high. We had gone through the only opening that didn't launch you onto rocks.

"That wasn't on the map," Gibson said.

"I know it wasn't." I said. "The platoon! Specht get that engine going now!" Specht was already working like a madman. "Everyone paddle up river back to the falls. We have to warn the rest of the boats."

Specht got the engine going after a minute and delivered us to the rock face at the side of the falls. Gibson and I climbed up the wall. Henneberry and Hilchey's boat was in the calm water not far from the falls. They were shocked to see Gibson and meappear out of no where. The visual perception from their end was very deceptive. Gibson and I yelled warnings and pointed to the only safe chute to take the falls. Henneberry and Hilchey's boat took the falls hard. Hilchey was at the controls of his boat and turned it back up river when they had recovered. They tossed me a safety rope. The other boats all took the falls no problem one at a time, except for Quickfall's boat which was last. It got stuck on the rocks and hung half over the falls. I threw one end of the rope to Corporal Todd who was in the front of Quickfall's boat and the other end to Warren Officer Hilchey. Hilchey gunned his boat and pulled Quickfall's boat off the rocks and over the falls.

We had all made it safely. A very dangerous situation had turned into an exciting one. Everyone pulled out their maps. No waterfall was marked. We had learned not to fully trust the maps. A good lesson in the Arctic.

We took a short rest while I and Sergeant Quickfall had a heart-to-heart talk. When we were off alone, I turned to face him.

"Your performance on this river has been unsatisfactory, Sergeant. Your crew puts no effort into their jobs and your boat has been hung up twice on rocks. The lives of you and your men depend on every member doing their jobs one hundred percent. There are no second chances in the Arctic. We are on our own up here. It's not a game. You get hung up one more time, or give me a reason to question you or your crew's performance, and I'll fire you as section commander, break up your boat crew, and re-assign all of you to other boats." I was very mad. "Is that clear?"

"Yes, sir!" Quickfall snapped. He was instinctively standing at attention.

"Good. Now pass the word to your crew. We move out in two minutes." Quickfall turned smartly and walked back to his boat. Heart-to-heart talks in the military are sometimes very one sided. This one was, but it worked. Quickfall's performance for the rest of our trip can only be rated as outstanding. He was a changed individual. The message had gotten through. He was enthusiastic and efficient. His men moved with more determination, and we were never delayed by them again.

The days on the river were great. Every turn brought new spectacular landscapes that took your breath away. The confidence of the men grew with each set of rapids. One day alone we shot twenty-three sets of rapids. The rapids we encountered were far larger and faster than anything we had encountered during our training at CFB Petawawa. We got very proficient at navigating rapids. I figured we could all get employment with a white-water rafting company easily.

We arrived at the portage point near the Burnside Falls and pulled off the river to make camp. We had reached the portage point safely and in the process had developed into a team. We had crossed the Arctic Circle on the river and had grown as individuals and as a group. We would need all our strength for what lay ahead.

Burnside Falls: Trial

The weather changed from the sunny days on the river to rain, cold, and high winds. As I stood in the pouring rain looking over our camp, I kept thinking about the lecture I had given back at CFB Petawawa to the men about the Arctic being a "desert-like climate" with very low annual precipitation. Sure; the one year I lead an expedition to the Arctic, it has the highest rainfall in fifty years!

I was not looking forward to the four-mile portage, but wanted to get underway as soon as possible. Captain Henneberry had other ideas. He had been studying the map and found a long curving beach that, if we could get to, would cut our portage down to only two miles. It was very tempting to cut our portage in half, given the amount of equipment we had to haul overland. Captain Henneberry suggested we do an extensive reconnoiter of the Burnside gorge and falls area and keep an open mind. I was suspicious of his intentions.

On the reconnoiter I took every boat commander and everyone in a command position. I wanted everyone to see first hand the area and wanted their input. Off we trekked. The reconnoiter was very detailed and took about five hours. I didn't like what I saw. From our current position to the falls, the Burnside River moved into a long, twisting, narrow gorge. The gorge walls are eighty to one hundred feet of sheer rock. The river raged below with a power and rapids I had never seen before. At the narrowest point (let's call this point "the gap"), the gorge was only about twelve feet across; Captain Henneberry and I climbed down to examine the gap carefully. At the river base, the noise was incredible and the rapids were six to ten feet high. The river widened slightly after the gap area and eventually came to the long curving beach.

Just beyond the beach was the first of the two Burnside water falls. The water plunged eighty feet at the first main falls and continued on to a second falls of only about twenty feet in height. The twenty-foot falls were impossible to live through (assuming you survived the first) since they hit a rock face at the bottom and turned ninety degrees. The distance from the gap to the main falls was about one kilometer.

When we got back to camp, Captain Henneberry, Warrant Officer Hilchey, Sergeant Gibson, and I went into our tent to discuss the situation. What followed left me in a state of shock—Captain Henneberry wanted to go for the beach. He thought we could easily make it and we would cut our portage in half. Henneberry wanted to hear our opinions. Warrant Officer Hilchey was willing to try it on his own, but was not willing to subject the men to it. In his opinion it was too dangerous for the men. Sergeant Gibson did not want to try it at all. "Far too dangerous," he said. I was against the idea totally. I did not want to risk any of my men in the gorge. It was too dangerous. The discussion ended.

"You have not convinced me of the dangers," Captain Henneberry said. "I think we can do it and we will. I am the senior ranking individual on this expedition, and I will take full and total responsibility for anything that happens." The shock was total.

"Could you say that again, sir?" Warrant Officer Hilchey said.

"I said, we are going to do it and I'll take full responsibility," Captain Henneberry said.

Henneberry was our safety officer. I did not feel very safe. Captain Henneberry was the senior officer on the expedition (I was a Lieutenant), and he had given us a direct order.

In the military, you follow orders. Reporting the situation to higher headquarters was impossible since we were out of radio contact. That left only two options. Option one: follow the order. Option two: refuse to obey the order and (more important than my safety) refuse to allow the men under my command to follow it. This option would have meant a number of things: effectively taking over, removing Captain Henneberry from any position of authority (by force if necessary), and of course, facing a court marshal when I returned to civilization. Some choice.

After much agonizing, I did only thing I thought I could do. I obeyed the order. We were going to go down the gorge.

Now the job was to develop a plan and issue the orders to the platoon. I had to issue the orders as though I was one hundred percent convinced of the plan's success. Any doubt on my part would have an adverse affect on the troop's morale and ability to achieve the mission.

The plan was relatively simple. We tied empty gas cans on the outside of each boat to cushion the impact against the gorge walls when we tried to go through the gap. Radio communication was impossible in the gorge, so we were to depart from the portage point at five-minute intervals. Captain Henneberry's and Warrant Officer Hilchey's boat was to lead off. Their job was to get through the gap and stop just behind it to act as a safety boat in case of an emergency. The second boat down the river would be my boat. I was to go down through the gap and to the beach where I was to act as a safety boat. All the other boats were to follow at five-minute intervals. Sounds easy, right? We found out it was not a good plan.

All was set except for the weather. We had to wait for the rain to stop in order to dry out our equipment a little before packing it away. We waited twenty-four hours before the weather cooperated. I had a very bad feeling about the situation. I spent considerable time in prayer asking God's deliverance and safety for all of my men. The time finally came; we loaded the boats and prepared to leave.

Captain Henneberry's and Warrant Officer Hilchey's boat left the portage point and headed down the river. I had five minutes. Sergeant Gibson and I were in the front of the boat, with Corporals Marshal and Specht at the back. Corporal Specht was at the engine controls. These were our regular seats and I didn't want to disrupt the routine at this critical moment. Sergeant Gibson looked at me and shook his head.

"I have a bad feeling about this," Gibson whispered to me. "I didn't sleep at all last night. Something is going to happen. I can feel it."

"Yeah. I can feel it too," I said. "This is not going to be good."

"I'm really scared about going into that gorge," Gibson said.

"Scared? I passed that point a long time ago. I'm terrified. I can hear the waterfall from here," I said.

"Time, sir," Sergeant Quickfall said. "Good luck."

I turned to him and the men and gave the thumbs up signal. I saw Corporal Todd looking at me doubtfully.

"Take it easy, Todd. Nothing to it, this is a piece of cake!" I said.

Todd smiled and shook his head at my bravado. "I hope so, sir," he said as my boat started moving down river.

"Don't worry! I'll see you later!" I yelled.

Todd gave me the thumbs up. I looked forward to concentrate on the situation. We were moving very fast through large rapids. I signaled directions and positioning to Corporal Specht at the controls.

"Keep the boat straight, Specht!" I yelled back over the roar of the water. Into the gorge and around the first turn. The second turn and then the gap were coming on fast. As we rounded the second turn, the boat moved sideways down river.

"Straighten her out, Specht!" I yelled.

"I'm trying!" Specht yelled back. We were clearly around the corner and heading for the gap. I couldn't believe what I saw—Captain Henneberry was standing on a gentle slope before the gap taking pictures of us. Taking pictures! He was the *safety* officer who was supposed to be in the *safety* boat. I felt real safe! I heard Corporal Marshal yell a warning and suddenly the boat flipped over!

Military engineering officers will tell you that it is impossible to flip a 15-man rubber assault boat, especially one that is fully loaded. We did the impossible. I would have felt proud, but I was a little preoccupied at that moment. I was taken totally off guard; I was suddenly in the water upside down. My right leg had gotten caught in the guide line on the outside of the boat and I was being dragged down the river upside down. The air was knocked out of me when we hit the freezing water. I gasped in a mouthful of water. Breathing was a habit I had gotten used to.

Adrenaline surged through my veins and things moved in slow motion. The Burnside falls were less than one kilometer away. Time to act. *Now!* I reached up blindly to my caught right foot and untangled it. Still hanging on to the guide line, I pulled my head above the water line. Air. Beautiful air. I coughed and saw Corporal Marshal beside me hanging on to the boat.

"Everyone okay?" I yelled.

"Yeah," Corporal Specht yelled from the other side of the boat.

"Where is Gibson?" I asked.

"I don't know, he's not here!" Specht replied.

Great. I'm missing my medical Sergeant, when certain people will require medical attention shortly—assuming they live. One of them being me.

"Hang on to the boat! We're going to get out of here!" I yelled. Get out of here? How? Gibson decided to join the party at that moment and popped up gagging and coughing near Corporal Marshal and me. I was glad Gibson had returned. I remembered specifically sending him an invitation to the party. We reached out, grabbed him, and held him close to the boat. He was in rough shape.

While I was checking out the river bottom upside down, we had obviously shot through the gap because we were now in calmer water behind it. We were still progressing rapidly towards the falls.

Meanwhile, we had disrupted Warrant Officer Hilchey's day as the flipped boat shot by him. He was at the controls of the safety boat and raced by us. I felt like waving, but didn't want to let go of Gibson *or* the boat. Warrant Officer Hilchey drove his boat at full speed by us, turned his boat back up river and came at us. He rammed us hard and I was knocked under water again. When I came up, I realized what he was doing. He had rammed us against the wall of the gorge and was holding us there. We scrambled out of the water at the base of the gorge on a tiny ledge.

We were safe. Well, relatively anyway. Time to try to save our boat. Warrant Officer Hilchey had two other people in his boat, Corporals Warner and Mace. Corporal Mace was petrified with fear and was of no help the entire time. Corporal Warner threw us a rope, which we attached to our boat. Our boat started moving back into the rapids again. We had to let go of the rope or go swimming for a second time. The river was too strong. Corporal Warner was attaching a second rope to our boat when he was dragged into the water. Warrant Officer Hilchey was watching us and missed Warner going in the water.

"Warner!" I yelled at Hilchey and pointed. "Get Warner!" Hilchey turned and saw Warner being sucked under the boat by the force of the rapids. Hilchey left the controls of his engine and jumped over the massive load of equipment in his boat. He reached down and tried to pull Warner out but failed. Then I saw an amazing feat of strength. Hilchey reached down again and pulled Warner out of the water and almost clean over his head. Warner weighed about 175 pounds, but ended up on top of the pile of equipment in the centre of the boat.

Hilchey turned and jumped back over the equipment to the engine, which had stopped. The last I saw of Hilchey, his crew and boats, he was madly trying to start his engine as our boat was dragging his boat rapidly down the rapids towards the falls. They disappeared around the next corner out of sight.

I quickly turned to assess our situation. Four of us clung to the base of an eighty-foot gorge wall on a ledge about two feet wide. The river raged by us. It was getting dark. The wind was howling through the cannon and we were suffering varying degrees of hypothermia. Sergeant Gibson was in the worst condition of all. He had no feeling in his arms and legs and was in shock. After thinking it over, I'd have to classify this as a bad day.

"This is great!" Corporal Specht yelled over the noise.

"Specht, if this is your idea of a good time, you're crazier than I am," I yelled back.

"Impossible sir!" He had me there. "I was just trying to look on the bright side."

"Bright side?" I asked.

"Sure," he looked at his watch, "by now we could have been going over the falls!"

"Oh, that bright side," I said. I was very concerned that Hilchey and his crew had gone over the falls with our boat. "Would you like to lead us in a sing along?"

"Okay," Specht said smiling.

Marshal had been studying the rock face. "Sir!" Marshal said.

"Yeah," I said.

"I can make this climb," Marshal said.

Oh no, the insanity was spreading! I looked up. "What do you mean?" I asked.

"I can climb this. I'm a rock climber; it's a hobby of mine. I've done a lot worse climbs. This is no problem," he said. No problem? I looked up again. Was help on the way? I had no idea. There was no sign of Captain Henneberry or anyone else. Gibson couldn't hang on for ever. He needed to get warm quickly or I'd loose him.

"Are you sure?" I asked.

"Yes, sir," Marshal replied confidently.

"Okay, give it a try, but be careful. Don't push it. If you get in trouble, come back down. Got it?" I asked.

"Yeah, no sweat, sir." Marshal smiled.

He started climbing up the rock face. He moved slowly picking his foot and hand holds carefully. Marshal tested each hold prior to putting his weight on it. He was very good and he made it to the top. I started to breath again. Specht cheered.

"Sir!" Marshal yelled from the top. "I'll go get help, you guys hang on!" He then disappeared.

Three of us were left on the ledge. It was bitterly cold now. It was getting darker. Specht and I told jokes and tried to keep Gibson alert. We waited.

"Sir," Marshal yelled.

"Yeah, Marshal," I yelled back.

"I met Captain Henneberry and some other guys coming up. We have ropes. I'll throw one down. Loop it around your shoulders and we'll pull you up one at a time."

"Okay," I said. A little while later one end of a rope sailed down to us. Specht and I secured it around Gibson and gave the all clear. Sergeant Gibson couldn't help the team on top of the gorge much. They hauled him up the eighty feet. Two of us were now on the ledge. The end of the rope returned.

"Sir, you go next," Specht said. "You're cold."

"No, Specht. Thanks, but you're next," I said.

"I'm okay, sir," He said.

"No, Specht, you're going, that's an order," I said firmly.

He put the rope around himself. I signaled the all clear. Up he went. One left on the ledge. A ledge in the Burnside gorge is a lonely place. It was extremely cold and very dark now.

The rope came down a final time. I slipped it around me, checked it, and gave the all clear. Up I started to climb. I was worried about how tired the guys were getting up top. The last ten feet were sheer rock with no hand holds. Master-Corporal Kolmer popped his head over the top.

"Hi sir, time for Batman," He said. Batman? In the Arctic?

"What?" I asked.

"You know, walk up the wall with your feet." This was relying totally on their brute strength to pull me up.

"Alright, Kolmer, but don't tell Robin I was having fun without him," I said. I walked up the last ten feet. It was not the best impersonation of Batman, since I had left my mask and cape at home, but I made it to the top. I was the coldest I have ever been in my life. I had been on the ledge an hour and five minutes.

I shook everyone's hands, even Captain Henneberry's. He told me he had seen our boat flip over and ran and warned the rest of the platoon off the river. Captain Henneberry was worried about my boat and the equipment in it.

"I don't care about the equipment. I need you to find Warrant Officer Hilchey and his crew. The last I saw, my boat was dragging them towards the falls," I said. I value human life over equipment any day.

Captain Henneberry took Master-Corporal Kolmer and one other man to search down river. I took my boat crew and walked back up river to find out where the rest of my platoon was. The four of us paraded off with me leading. We were all wrapped in emergency blankets and looked like a parade of monks going to a church service.

I found Sergeant Quickfall and his crew and another boat (Master-Corporal Kolmer's) on my side of the river. There were eleven of us total. The rest of my platoon was on the other side of the river. When the signal to get off the river had come, they had all frantically driven to the nearest shore. We were very spread out up and down the river. There was no way across the river due to the size of the rapids, without ending up going down the gorge.

It was too risky to re-join the platoon. Sergeant Quickfall and his crew were glad to see us alive.

"Sir, when we heard a boat had flipped, we should have guessed it would be yours," Quickfall said.

"You know me Quickfall, I'm always the first in, even to swimming parties," I said. I saw Corporal Todd smiling at me. "How's it going, Todd?"

"I was going to ask you that question, sir," Todd said.

"Never worry about me, Todd. I told you it was a piece of cake and I'd see you later." He continued to shake his head in disbelief.

I began to think that my men just followed me to find out what would happen next. "Sergeant Quickfall, get a tent out and put everyone, but one sentry, to bed. See that my crew gets something hot to drink and eat, and dry clothes."

"Right away, sir," Quickfall said. There was a gaggle of my men on the opposite shore just standing there staring at me. This was a classic situation where a crisis happens and everyone stands around waiting for someone to tell them what to do. I yelled and made gestures towards the radio.

Eventually, Sergeant Martin got the message and he picked up the radio handset.

"Martin, how many men do you have with you?" I asked.

"I have sixteen men in total, counting me, sir," Martin said. With lightning-fast math (I counted on my fingers twice because my brain was still frozen): eleven in my group, sixteen in Martin's group, three in Henneberry's group, and three in Hilchey's group (I hoped). Total of thirty-three persons, everyone accounted for. It was now totally dark.

"Okay, Martin, everyone is accounted for. I want you to put one man on sentry and one on radio watch and then put everyone else to bed. Tomorrow will be a long day." I then signed off.

Later, everyone in my group was in bed as I sat up on radio watch. I couldn't sleep. Sergeant Gibson was shook up, but he was okay. He had been under water for about thirty yards. Not the most enjoyable experience in the world. I had Quickfall check the amount of rations we had. Three days' worth. In addition we had only one battery for the radio left, which was about to die on me. Any minute now I would be out of radio contact with the other groups and in three days we would be out of food. With each passing moment, concern for Hilchey and his crew grew. I waited.

"Niner, this is Niner Alpha, do you read over." The radio crackled weakly. It was Hilchey! The voice was low and full of static, but it was definitely Hilchey. I grabbed the handset.

"Hilchey, are you and the men okay?" I asked.

"Yes. I got the engine going and had to cut the rope attached to your boat because it was about to drag us over the falls. We made the beach but your boat is gone." I really didn't give a care about my boat at that moment.

"Okay listen," I made sure Martin was on the line as well, "we will all start the portage at first light from our current positions. Hilchey, I have only three days rations and no radio batteries. We need a re-supply. We will all rendezvous at the base of the second Burnside falls in three days. Acknowledge." They both acknowledged that they understood. "This is my last transmission; see you in three days, good luck." I signed off. I was glad to hear from Hilchey. The radio gave a final hiss and died. I felt very alone. Leadership is a lonely business. I prayed to God and gave him thanks for saving everyone's life. I put my head down and eventually drifted into restless sleep.

. . .

The next three days were physically brutal. We were off the main portage route and had to go through low bog, up a very high hill, through low ground again and finally up onto a ridge and to the second falls. Everyone slept three hours. Two soldiers were on sentry duty each night and their job was to move small items forward. Our team moved forward constantly, one hundred meters at a time. I only had the clothes on my back and no bug net. The flies tormented me mercilessly. All of our feet had gone soft from sitting for long periods in the boats and being wet continually for the past three weeks. Blisters and more blisters. We made it. We moved thousands of pounds of equipment over extremely rough terrain in three days. Not one man quit or complained. I was never so proud of my men.

At the end of the portage, I allowed Sergeant Gibson to inspect my feet. I didn't allow him near my feet before the end of the portage, since I knew he would prevent me from carrying my share of the load of equipment. I couldn't quit despite the agony of the blisters. I couldn't let down my men. Gibson said that my feet were the worst feet he had ever seen. I had ripped the soles off of both feet and by the end of the portage could barely walk. Sergeant Gibson was mad and told me that I as not allowed to lift anything heavier than a canteen to my mouth from now on.

At the bottom of the second falls, Warrant Officer Hilchey met us on schedule with more food and radio batteries. We found some of our equipment washed up on shore. Sergeant Gibson recovered all of his personal kit, and Corporals Marshal and Specht recovered some of their kit. I only recovered my sleeping bag and bug net everything else was lost.

A search of the area uncovered our boat stuck in an eddy at the base of the second falls. The boat was still intact and inflated! It had survived going over two water falls, but all of the equipment had been stripped off it. I lead a "boat rescue" team down a rocky climb to the base of the falls. Warrant Officer Hilchey was on the other side of the river and threw a rope to us to attach to the boat. Hilchey, with the help of several others, pulled the boat out of the eddy and into the main current and let it go down river where we salvaged it. The boat was too dam-

aged and shredded to be ever used again, but the rescue was successful. My party then had to climb out of the area we were in. Sure, Sergeant Gibson made it out with our help, and Marshal (climber extraordinaire) made it look easy, but to me it was one hairy experience. It involved climbing onto a rock and then jumping up and grasping a hand hold on an overhang. Then you had to go from one hand hold to another, using hands only, as your feet swung freely in the air, up the overhang. My turn came, I jumped up and missed the hand hold with my right hand, but caught it with the finger tips of my left hand. As I hung in the air, suspended by the fingertips of one hand, looking down at the rocks below, it occurred to me that I had no experience in rock climbing. None! Not even the basics, and here I was leading rock climbing outings and pretending I was some sort of monkey. Hanging there was a poor place for reality to set in. I decided to pretend that I knew what I was doing and crawled up the overhang using hands only. You never know what you are capable of until you try.

The platoon was together again. It was really great seeing everyone. Our team felt whole again.

As a group, we loaded the boats and drove into the village of Bathurst Inlet. I think we were the most exciting thing to ever happen to Bathurst Inlet. The entire village turned out to watch the "army" arrive. Children cheered and ran along the shore with us. It was a crazy situation, but it felt wonderful when I stepped from my boat, like General MacArthur returning to the Philippines, and had to shake the hands of all the natives in the village. We had arrived in Bathurst Inlet in style.

Bathurst Inlet: Moving On

While my men and I were enduring the portage around the Burnside Falls, Captain Henneberry was searching for my boat and equipment and had called Yellowknife Headquarters from a radio the locals had to report the incident of the flipped boat and lost equipment.

Captain Todd (from Yellowknife) and his group of Rangers had arrived in the village of Bathurst Inlet with metal boats equipped with 65-horse-power engines. Captain Todd's group consisted of a regular force Sergeant and four Canadian Rangers. The word "Rangers" may be slightly misleading, if you confuse them with the American Rangers. American Rangers are an elite fighting force in the United States Army, specializing in small-unit patrol and strike missions (often suicidal in nature during war time). Now, the Canadian Rangers are not quite the same. They are native people who are given two weeks of training (weapons, drill and saluting are covered), a 303 rifle, two hundred rounds of ammunition per year, a Ranger arm band, a Ranger baseball cap, and a Ranger sweatshirt. Okay, so you can't equate the two types of Rangers based on the name "Ranger." The Canadian Rangers are an extremely useful resource in the military. They are used to work with and train southern soldiers in the ways of the north. There are a number of soldiers walking around who owe a debt to the Rangers who have saved them in search and rescue operations. Their knowledge of the north makes the Rangers indispensable.

The four Rangers consisted of three generations. Tom and Bill were in their mid to late thirties. They were knowledgeable about the north, and could fix and improvise any mechanical engine or machine (they couldn't fix the 515 set, no one is that good). They were the middle generation of Inuit who knew both the native, and the white man's world. Charlie was an elderly Inuit of undeterminable age. He looked like he was somewhere between forty and seventy. Charlie was the master of knowledge about the north. He knew where he was at all times (in a land that looked all the same to me), and had a wealth of knowledge about nature and its animals. Charlie was the old generation, which is unfortunately dying out. He knew only the native way and didn't need, or care about, the white man's way. If a machine Charlie was using broke, he would leave it where it broke down and would then work on getting a new one. Time as I knew it was meaningless to Charlie. Tomorrow could mean tomorrow, or the day after, or next week, or whenever—only Charlie knew for sure. This was a source of continual frustration for my big city, Southern, mindset. The last Ranger was Danny, who was eighteen years old. Danny represented the new generation and the tragedy of what the white man had done to the native people. Danny knew nothing about the north. Oh, he lived there, but he watched TV on satellite dish, played video games, and his sole ambition in life was to be a Florida beach bum. Danny, for some reason never made clear, had found himself in Miami, Florida, for a twenty-four-hour period at one point. He fell in love. The warmth (he hated the cold) and the beaches were forever stuck in his mind. Danny had lost his culture.

Major Beztilny, from the Headquarters in Toronto, and Brigadier-General Dodd, the commander of Northern Region Headquarters in Yellowknife, flew in on the Twin Otter aircraft to assess the situation. They asked a lot of questions, took statements, and made speeches about the great job we were doing. As soon as Major Beztilny and the General left, we took off in the boats.

My boat crew, since we no longer had a boat, was assigned to Charlie's and Danny's boat. Charlie drove, while Danny sat in front with his long hair blowing in the wind. Charlie only knew two speeds, "full out" and "stop." We were soon far ahead of everyone else and I had to convince him to go back once every hour or so to find the rest of the group. Once found, we would turn around and take off again. At one point, we were flying along, and

Charlie suddenly killed the engine and grabbed his rifle. He turned and pointed the rifle in my direction. I didn't think I had done anything to upset him, but once again it was time for action. Sergeant Gibson and I dove for the floor of the boat, as Charlie fired over our heads as rapidly as he could. Danny had joined him in the firing spree. I was still cowering in the bottom of the boat when the firing stopped. I slowly got up and asked Charlie if Canada had been invaded and no one had bothered to advise me. It turned out that Charlie had seen a seal and decided to go hunting. Danny hadn't seen the seal but had joined in anyway. Lucky for the seal, Charlie wasn't a very good shot and it got away safely. I didn't turn my back on Charlie again.

We left the village and traveled up Bathurst Inlet. Captain Henneberry decided that we should attempt to reach Bay Chimo the first night. I arrived at Bay Chimo in Charlie's boat. The rest of the boats followed us in later. It became pitch black and two boats were missing, Captain Henneberry's and Sergeant Quickfall's boats. I prayed to God for their safe arrival.

"Master-Corporal Kolmer?" I yelled.

"Yes, sir?" he said in my ear. He was standing beside me on the shore. I jumped. I had been pre-occupied with staring out to sea and listening for signs of engine noise.

"Don't do that," I told him. He smiled. "I want you to take a man with you, grab a lantern and climb to high ground. Use the lantern to signal out to sea for Captain Henneberry."

"Yes, sir," Kolmer said and ran off.

I then went over to Captain Todd and we agreed to send Tom and Bill out in their boat to search for the missing people. They left immediately. The wind and waves had picked up. I paced the shore line while the rest of my men set up camp. After a long while, Tom and Bill returned.

"Well, where are they?" I asked.

"We can't find them," Tom said.

Todd joined us. I turned to him. "They have to go back out. My people are out there in the Arctic Ocean and there is a storm coming up." I was getting upset.

"Take it easy," Todd said.

"They've got to try again," I said. Todd took Tom aside. After a while, Tom shrugged his shoulders and agreed to go back out. Todd explained to me that the Inuit believe in a sort of fate. Tom had tried once and was willing to leave the survival of my people to fate. This was not my belief.

Tom came back for a second time and reported no sign of the missing boats. Two boats were missing in the Arctic Ocean with nine men on board. The storm was generating four-foot waves and it was a pitch black night with the low clouds obscuring any light from the stars or the moon. I paced the shore. Todd waited with me. Where were they? Did they capsize the boats in the ocean and drown? I continued to pace.

"Listen!" Todd said suddenly. I stopped pacing and listened. Yes, very quiet, but definitely an engine! "There!" Todd pointed as two rubber boats slowly made their way through the waves towards shore.

Relief! Thank God! When they arrived, Warrant Officer Hilchey told me that Quickfall's engine had started running at about one-quarter power. To make matters worse, the boat started leaking air (the glue in the patches was dissolving in the salt water of the ocean), and the boat started to take on water as the waves came over the top. Hilchey's boat had towed Quickfall's as the crew bailed for their lives. They could see the light we had put out for miles and it had acted as their navigation beacon. They were all glad to be on solid ground. By this time, the sea was very rough.

The next day, Captain Henneberry and my men put on another fire power demonstration. We burned off our ammunition (except for the hollow point rounds for our white four legged friends).

Captain Todd and I were talking to the Inuit Chief of Bay Chimo when I noticed Todd staring off to the distance with a concerned look. Suddenly, he took off running for the creek in the village at full speed and stripping off his clothes as he went. I turned and followed at a dead run not knowing where we were going. I had learned to trust Todd and I reacted immediately. As we got closer to the creek, I noticed a head bobbing in the water. The head had come up a third time and gone back under. It did not re-surface. Todd jumped into the freezing water and grabbed the boy, and swam back to the edge of the creek. I took the boy from Todd, stripped off my jacket and wrapped the boy in it.

The boy was coughing up water and shivering with cold. Todd climbed out and we walked back to the Chief. It turned out it was the Chief's son who had fallen in the creek. He couldn't swim. Captain Todd had saved the boy's life. I congratulated Todd on his heroism and later wrote a letter of commendation to Brigadier-General Dodd, the Commander of Northern Region Headquarters. Todd had done a tremendous job.

We were delayed in Bay Chimo due to a storm that was brewing. We spent a lot of time repairing equipment, talking, and playing cards.

The weather cleared slightly and we made a run up Bathurst Inlet. We were trying to make it to the Kent Peninsula, which would have given us an almost direct run across Dease Strait to Byron Bay, our final destination. We made it as far as a small island, Fisher Island, north of Bay Chimo, before the bad weather and high seas forced us ashore. I stood on the stone beach of Fisher Island and watched the strong cold northern winds whip the sea into vicious white caps of ten to twelve feet in height. We were stranded on a small island in the Arctic Ocean.

The Canadian Coast Guard

Once a year in the summer, the small settlements in the Arctic are re-supplied by freighter. How would you like to make a shopping list once a year? Don't forget anything. In order for the freighter to make it into some settlements, a Canadian Coast Guard ice breaker leads the way to ensure all ice is cleared away.

Tom had a very small radio (that worked) that he used to contact Bay Chimo. The Coast Guard had arrived at Bay Chimo after we had left.

"Use the Coast Guard," I said to Captain Todd. "We can tell them that we're conducting a hitchhiking tour of the Arctic and could use a lift to Byron Bay."

"Well, it's worth asking them." Todd agreed.

"I'm not sure how else we're going to get off this island."

"I'll ask, but the captain of the ice breaker may say he can't help us," Todd said.

"Tell the captain something from me, either he can assist us now or rescue us in two days when we run out of food," I said.

"Good point," Todd confirmed. Todd and Tom took off back to Bay Chimo. We ate lunch and waited. Eventually they returned. Todd got out of the boat, smiled, and gave me the thumbs up signal.

"The captain of the ice breaker C.C.G.S. *Camsell* sends his regards, and says that if we don't mention this to anyone, then he won't mention it to anyone. He'll be here tomorrow morning," Todd said. The Coast Guard had agreed to get us off the island. The storm continued.

The light of dawn had just broken the next morning when our sentry came to the command tent, woke us up, and told us the Coast Guard ship was about a mile off the island. The men ran to the shore, waved, and cheered. I got dressed quickly and ran out to watch a helicopter lift off the ship and fly towards us.

When the helicopter landed, the pilot shut it down. The pilot and his passenger got out as we walked over to meet them.

"Hi, I'm Lieutenant Steve Gallant," I said, extending my hand to the passenger.

"Hi, David Stowe," he said as we shook. "I'm the first officer of the *Camsell*. We heard you guys could use a lift."

"We could use a lot of things, but a lift to Byron Bay would be great." I agreed.

Introductions were then made all around. Over coffee, Stowe advised us that the helicopter would transport all our kit to the ship in a cargo net suspended under the helicopter. Warrant Officer Hilchey organized the men to break all our equipment into equal-size bundles. The troops would go out to the ship in their boats, climb up a cargo net draped over the side of the *Camsell*, and on to its deck. A crane on the *Camsell* would lift each boat on to the deck.

We moved quickly and the gear was transported to the *Camsell* in less than an hour. I was on the last boat out to the *Camsell*. The rain was constant, winds cold and strong, and the waves in the ocean were very high. It reminded me of a very wet roller coaster ride, but with considerable danger attached. We would not have lasted long in the frigid Arctic waters if a boat capsized. The *Camsell* seemed to be a long way out, but we made it. Climbing the cargo net was lots of fun (strange things excite me). I only lost my footing once on the slippery net.

When all the boats were loaded, Stowe took me to the bridge to meet the captain.

"Captain Gord Graham, welcome aboard the Canadian Coast Guard ice breaker *Camsel*," he said. I looked up at a bear of a man with a hand twice my size. Graham had a weathered face of a man who had spent his life at sea. His presence commanded immediate respect.

"Lieutenant Steve Gallant, Canadian Armed Forces." I said. "Nice of you to pick up my pack of strays Captain."

"Glad we could be of assistance. How did the

army end up stranded on an island in the Arctic Ocean?" Graham asked.

I explained about our mission and how we had gotten to Fisher Island.

"How long have you been up in the Arctic?" Graham asked.

"Thirty-one days." I said.

"Well, if you can pry yourself away from the bridge, I can offer you a shower," Graham said.

I turned to him quickly. "A shower?" I asked.

"And breakfast," Graham added.

"Breakfast? You mean with real food?"

He nodded.

"Not boil in the bag omelets that taste like rubber?"

He nodded again.

"I'm with you." He led the way off the bridge and towards the ship's galley.

When we got to the galley, my men were finishing up their breakfast and heading for showers. We all ate until we thought we would burst and the showers were fantastic. I learned that the *Camsell* was on her final voyage through the Arctic and was due to be de-commissioned and sold for scrap.

What a sorry end to the vessel that plucked us from a desperate situation, provided us with four hours of civilization and comfort, and gave us passage to Byron Bay.

The big event of the trip was the first officer allowing me to steer the ship. I stood on the bridge, white knuckled grip on the big wheel, watching the compass heading, and trying to follow the instructions of the first officer who was looking over my shoulder. An experienced sailor I'm not. I steered for twenty thrilling minutes through the raging Arctic Ocean with waves crashing over the bow of the ship. It was great. I was ready to enlist in the Coast Guard until I went down to check on my men. Three quarters of them were very green and sea sick. I didn't tell anyone I had come from the bridge and steering the ship.

Before we arrived at Byron Bay, we had a quick lunch for those with cast iron stomachs. I ate heartily. The first officer advised us that the seas were too rough, and we could not put the boats over the side to make our own way to shore. The only solution was to deflate the boats and trans-

port them by helicopter along with the gear and my men. Everyone got a helicopter ride.

I said thanks and goodbye to Captain Graham and his crew. Then I had to say goodbye to Captain John Todd and his party. Charlie was finally rid of us and going home in style on the Camsell. I had grown to like Todd and would miss his calm, cool manner. All my men and equipment were ashore. I stepped into the waiting helicopter, waved, and lifted off for Byron Bay.

Byron Bay: Success

As the helicopter touched down at Byron Bay, I felt a tremendous sense of accomplishment and relief. We had made it to our final destination in the Arctic. We had not made the trip according to the original plan, formulated hundreds of miles to the south, but then, plans never work out exactly as they are originally designed. You do your preparation, planning, and training, and then you begin. The theory stops at the starting line. The real test is how you deal with the obstacles encountered on route. Nothing worthwhile, or valued, is accomplished easily.

Byron Bay is a Defence Early Warning (DEW) Station. A DEW station is a radar sight manned by Canadian civilian technicians and supplied by the United States Air Force. The stations, which are strung out in a line across the Canadian Arctic, give early warning in the event of a missile or air attack by Russia.

The manager and crew at Byron Bay were very generous and glad to have company. DEW stations are lonely places at the best of times. They put us up in an airplane hangar with a platform at one end. We were not in tents for the first time in thirty-one days, and we were off the ground. To us, the hanger was like being in a high-class Hilton hotel. They also allowed us to have daily showers and gave us a big dinner. After what we had just experienced, these were extraordinary luxuries. We were really getting spoiled. The western world takes so many things for granted; you only notice the daily comforts of life and miss them when they are gone.

Warrant Officer Hilchey kept the men busy cleaning, repairing, and packing our equipment. I spent long hours writing letters of assessment on each member of my platoon. Captain Henneberry

put in several calls to our headquarters to advise them we had arrived on schedule and needed the two C130 Hercules aircraft to take us back home.

The first C130 arrived on schedule, but the second plane developed engine trouble and was diverted to another location. Only part of my platoon could go on the first plane. I wanted to stay and leave with the last of my men, but Captain Henneberry ordered me on to the plane. I reluctantly got on board. We took all we could, but left Sergeant Gibson and nine other men at Byron Bay to wait for the second plane.

Air Force pilots are amazing. When they don't want to do something, they pull out the old rule book, and quote obscure regulations about why they can't do what you need done. On the other hand, when they want to do something they throw away the old rule book and do it. A classic display of this generic trait of pilots was displayed at Byron Bay. One of the four engines of our C130 would not start up when we were about to take off. The pilots pulled out the old rule book and quoted some obscure meaningless dribble about why we were stuck in Byron Bay. They shut down the plane and asked me where the hotel was. I pointed to the hanger we were staying in. After they realized I was serious, the crew went into a huddle. The huddle broke up and the old rule book disappeared. There was no way the Air Force was going to spend a night in Byron Bay without proper hotel facilities with steaks and champagne. It took the fly boys forty-five minutes to get that fourth engine started, but they did it. We took off and flew south. Air Force, they are amazing.

Once back at CFB Petawawa, I went into frenzied activity. The Air Force claimed that they couldn't schedule another C130 to pick up the rest of my platoon at Byron Bay for another week to ten days. I did a lot of pounding on desks, and nasty phone calls to headquarters. I told everyone that my men only had one day's worth of food left and were going to starve to death. The Air Force reluctantly rescheduled a flight and brought Sergeant Gibson and the rest of my men home two days later. They only had one day's food left, but unknown to me, the DEW station people were feeding them like kings. My group didn't want to leave!

Back Home

We were united again as a group in CFB Petawawa.
Two days were spent turning in all the equipment,
handing out letters of assessment, getting everyone
paid, and having a party.

The party was a sober, sad affair. We had gone
to the Arctic, overcome life and death situations
withstood hardships, seen incredible sights, and
accomplished a 550 kilometer expedition that most
people would rate as difficult or impossible. Looking back, I can see God's mighty hand and great
salvation throughout. For thirty-three days we were
almost totally isolated and had to bond together as

a team for our survival. Now, despite the great success and pride we felt, we had to part and go our separate ways.

The next day I said goodbye to each man. I had taken a group of boys to the Arctic and returned with a group of men. Every commander always has, "his" platoon. The platoon he always remembers and longs to return too. These men will always be "my" platoon. The faces of Hilchey, Gibson, Quickfall, Kolmer, Specht, Marshal, Todd, and the others, will always be with me.

A short time after arriving back home, I put Warrant Officer Hilchey in for the Medal of Bravery for his courageous actions at the Burnside gorge. I am totally convinced that Hilchey risked his life to save the lives of five others. The Board of Officers that passes judgment on these things decided to downgrade my recommendation to a Chief of Defence Staff Commendation.

With God's help, I had made it through the river.

Part II
Through The Fire

Fire

Moving is not my favourite activity. My brother, being a kind, thoughtful, considerate person, came up with a unique solution: set fire to the house! Suddenly all the moving problems are solved. You just get in the car in your pajama bottoms and drive away. Easy. My brother, a really great guy. If you need help moving, I'll send him around to visit.

Mike is my younger bother. We were renting a house together in the outskirts of town. Eight months after moving in, the landlord sold the house and promised the new owner vacant possession (despite a signed one-year lease). We were told to move.

After the landlord left, I spent a couple of hours worrying about the necessary logistical arrangements required for moving. Getting boxes, packing dishes, glasses, pots, pans, cutlery, clothes, books, games, and pictures. Then comes renting the truck, dolly, blankets, organizing friends to help move and ensuring there are drinks and pizza available. Overall, it is a tremendous hassle. One of life's painful experiences that keeps reoccurring. Why I bothered worrying and planning those silly details I'll never understand. Mike arrived home shortly and his solution was close at hand.

"Our landlord visited today," I told Mike when he walked in the door. He had been out playing hockey and dropped his equipment in the doorway.

"What did he want?" Mike asked.

"He delivered this eviction notice." I handed Mike the letter and he read it as he reached into the fridge to get a drink.

"Garbage." Mike had passed his verdict. He threw the letter on the kitchen table. "Not worth the paper it's written on. We have a one-year lease. He can't throw us out just because he sold the property."

"Yeah, I agree," I said. "But eventually we will have to move. The only question is how long and how much effort do we want to spend on fighting this notice?"

"We'll stay until our one-year lease is up. His deal on the house will fall through unless he wants to buy out our lease?"

"Well, we should start thinking about finding a place and moving," I told him. "I'm going to bed. I'm exhausted. See you tomorrow." I headed upstairs to my room. I set my alarm clock, changed into my pajama bottoms (I don't wear the tops), and went to bed. I was asleep as soon as my head hit the pillow. It had been a long day, but the night would be longer.

A couple of hours later, God woke me up. I went from a very sound sleep to bolt upright in bed. I looked through my bedroom door and saw moving light. Up, out of my bed, down the stairs and into the kitchen.

Half of the kitchen was engulfed in flames.

Adrenaline started to pump through my blood stream. My world started to move in slow motion. My mind was working a mile a minute, but my body was responding at a turtle's pace (or so I thought). Time seemed to stand still. There was no panic. There was a certain amount of fear generated by the destructive power of the fire and the potential personal danger, but the overwhelming sensation was that of excitement. Excitement not in the sense of fun, but rather in that this was action! There was no time to panic, no time to have a debate, no time to form a committee and have meetings. The situation called for pure decisive action. After working in a bank for two years, with its mundane daily routine, this was exciting. I knew that my actions would have a dramatic impact on my own life and that of my brother. Our continued existence was resting on my shoulders.

Of course, having said all of the above, I was amazed at my thought processes. A fire extinguisher would have been really useful at that moment, but I didn't own one. *Water!* No, water wouldn't work. The source of the fire became evident immediately. There was a pot of oil raging away on the stove.

Water would have only help spread the burning oil. Turn off the stove to reduce the heat on the oil! (This was silly, but the mind works in mysterious ways in stressful situations). After three attempts at turning off the burner under the pot of oil and being driven back due to the tremendous heat, I gave up on the idea. Turn off the electricity in the house! No, the fuse box was downstairs in the basement and with the fire spreading very fast there was a good chance that I would get trapped without an escape route. I had run out of options. *Get Mike out and call the fire department!*

"Mike! Mike! Fire!" I yelled over the noise of the fire. I yelled several more times when he finally appeared in the stairway. Mike stood in his underwear, looking at me very confused and rubbing sleep from his eyes. "Fire! Get out of the house now! I'll call the fire department!" I yelled. Of course, as brothers always do, he ignored me. Mike turned around and ran up the stairs. Great! "Mike, get out of the house now!" I yelled again. No time for further discussion. The fire was spreading rapidly. I ran to the phone in the living room.

Fire department. What was the number? The

911 emergency services had not come to the neighborhood yet. I did not know the fire department's telephone number. Great. Phone book. *Where is the phone book? On the kitchen counter.* I looked back into the kitchen. Yup, there was the phone book alright. Phone books burn well. Great. The Operator. Of course, she can connect me. I dialed zero. *Time to clam down and talk in a normal relaxed voice.*

"Operator, May I help you?" A female voice answered on the second ring.

"Yes, Operator, I was wondering if you could possibly connect me with the fire department please?" I asked in a pleasant voice. Half of the kitchen was on fire.

"That number is available in your directory," she replied.

"Yes, I know that, Operator, but my directory is unreadable at the moment." I said glancing towards the kitchen.

"Sir, you can dial 411 for directory assistance and they will gladly provide you with the appropriate number."

What? I couldn't believe this. Obviously calm, cool, and collected was not making it. The kitchen was progressing well. Time for a little emotion. "Operator, my house is burning down around my ears!" I raised my voice on the phone. Then in a clam voiced I said, "I would consider it a personal favour, if you would connect me to the fire department."

"Sir," she said, unruffled, "is this an emergency?" The kitchen was now three-quarters on fire.

"Yes, Operator, I would consider this an emergency." I replied.

"Well," she sounded very indignant, "why didn't you say so? I'll connect you immediately."

The line when dead for a moment and then a male voice came on the line. "Fire Department," he said.

"Yes, I'd like to report a fire," and I gave my address.

The male voice repeated the address. "Is that a house or apartment?" he asked.

"A house," I responded.

"Could I have your name?" he asked.

I glanced into the kitchen. It was becoming habit forming as the flames got closer and closer to where I was on the phone. The ceiling was now on fire. I provided my name.

"Could I have your phone number, sir?"

Phone number? Something in the ceiling was causing tremendous black smoke to spread everywhere. I started to cough and crouched on to the floor. "Phone number?" I asked. "Why do you need my phone number?" *Cough.*

"It is Fire Department policy to verify all calls." *Cough, cough.* Calm and control had failed me again.

"Look it, buddy," I said raising my voice, "don't bother calling back to verify the call because no one will be around to answer the phone! Just send the fire trucks!" *Cough, cough.*

There was a momentary pause on the other end of the line. "Sir, are you by chance in the vicinity of the fire?" he asked, a little concerned.

I shared his concern. *Cough.* My eyes were watering badly.

"If you consider four feet the *vicinity,* then the answer is a definite yes!"

"Sir, I must ask that you vacate the premises immediately." He was very concerned now. I guess

normal callers aren't often within arms reach of the fire when they call into report a fire.

"Good idea?" I said as I hung up the phone. Time to "vacate." I was coughing badly and could not see clearly. The entire kitchen and back hallway were now on fire, and thick black smoke filled the house.

Where was Mike? Last I saw of him, he was running back upstairs in his underwear. I had to find him. Crouching down low, I half crawled/half ran through the smoke- filled, blazing kitchen, down the back hallway, and crashing through the back door. In a fit of coughing, I almost ran into Mike on the back porch. He was now wearing a pair of jeans. For him, modestly seemed to dominate personal survival. He had run back upstairs to his bedroom to recover his jeans and his wallet.

"You okay?" he asked. I continued coughing for a minute, or so, before I could answer.

"Slightly singed around the edges, but other than that I'm okay," I replied. I stood there in my pajama bottoms with bare feet, looking at him. "I know this may seem like a silly question, but why did you leave a pot of oil on the stove and go to bed?"

"It was an accident," He replied. "I was going to cook up some French fries, but I got tired and went to bed instead. I forgot to turn the pot of oil off."

A burst of flames came out the back door at us. We jumped back together.

"Let's get off this porch," Mike said.

Fire Department to the Rescue

Mike and I walked around to the front of the house to the driveway.

"Did you call the fire department?" Mike asked.

"Yeah," I said.

Mike cocked his ear towards the house. "Is that our telephone ringing?" Mike asked.

"Yeah, it's probably the fire department calling back to verify the call," I told him.

"You're kidding?" he asked.

"I wish I was," I said.

"I'm cold," Mike said. It was a cool October night.

"Why don't you get in the car to stay warm?" I suggested. Mike got into the car and remained there for the duration, while I waited for the fire trucks.

A couple of neighbors came out and asked if the house was on fire. When I confirmed that it was, they got excited and ran to tell others. That night I met neighbors I had never seen before. Everyone from a ten-block radius showed up. Someone could have set up a hot dog stand and made a fortune. A couple of the neighbors asked if anyone was still inside. I assured them that everyone was out of the house. My next door neighbor was very kind and ran and got me and Mike sweaters and some old running shoes to wear. They were about four sizes too big, but I was very grateful since I was shaking from the cold night air.

A car screeched to a halt at the bottom of our driveway and a guy jumped out very excited. "Is this where the fire is?" he yelled.

"Yeah!" I yelled back. He turned and ran into the street yelling. "The fire is here, the fire is here!"

Two other cars then came tearing down the road and screeched to a stop in front of the house. The drivers jumped out, one with an axe and the other with a fire extinguisher for a car. Talk about enthusiastic neighbors! These three guys started running all over the place yelling at each other. One broke the kitchen window with his axe and another turned on my garden hose that sprayed only a trickle of water. The other man with the fire extinguisher ran to the back of the house and contemplated using the extinguisher until he saw that the entire back of the house was engulfed in flames. He became discouraged and walked back to join his buddies. Curiosity had overcome me while watching this performance, so I approached them.

"Excuse me," I said, "who are you guys?"

One stuck out his chest, smiled, and stepped forward. "We're the volunteer fire department," he replied proudly.

"You're the fire department?" I asked and they nodded. "Shouldn't you guys have a fire truck or something?" They exchanged glances and looked a little embarrassed.

"We think the fire truck is lost," one said.

"You lost your fire truck?" I asked.

"Well," pause, "it will be here any moment," he said with as much confidence as he could muster. Great! "We're a composite unit," he explained, "part volunteer, part regular firefighters. The regular guys…"

"The guys with the fire truck?" I offered.

"Yeah," he was embarrassed, "we think they went the wrong way on Finch Avenue."

At that moment, the kitchen window totally shattered and flames jumped from it. They exchanged glances again. "We should wait on the road to direct the fire truck in." They then all shuffled out to the road. I shook my head. *I should have stayed in bed;* then again, I was glad I didn't as flames were now clearly visible in my bedroom window.

The fire truck eventually arrived. The three volunteer guys were so excited that they started jumping up and down. The Fire Chief, wearing his white hat, surveyed the situation and quickly called for two more units to the scene.

The firemen were good. A little slow off the mark, but they recovered quickly with very efficient firefighting. They had the fire under control within a few minutes of arrival, and mostly extinguished within thirty minutes of the other two fire trucks arrival.

The police and firemen both took statements from Mike and me. We told them the truth about how the fire started and the fire investigator later confirmed this.

The Fire Chief approached me. "Sorry about your loss, but we did the best that we could."

"You and your men did a great job when you finally got here," I assured him.

He became defensive. "When you called in the report the fire you should have said you were at Finch Avenue *East.*"

"East? But the street is called Finch Avenue. There is no east or west," I said.

"You should have specified Finch Avenue East." He was sticking to his story and laying the blame on me.

"Why did the volunteer firefighters know where to go?" I asked.

"You should have specified Finch Avenue East," The Chief was stating the official line, no compromise. He then surveyed the house again. "The insurance boys will have their work cut out for them."

I knew this would come up eventually. "Insurance?" I asked. "What insurance?"

The Chief turned and looked at me in disbelief. "You don't have insurance?" he asked.

"We tried three different insurance companies and not one of them would insure the place. They all said that the place was a fire trap."

The Chief looked over the charred house and back at me. "I guess they were right," he said.

"I'd like to go inside the house to see if I can get my car keys and try to salvage some important papers."

"You want to go in there?" he asked.

I nodded.

"It's dangerous in there."

I nodded again.

"Okay," he finally said.

The Chief felt sorry for me. He led the way and I followed him.

Aftermath

The Chief handed me a fireman's hat. I looked the funny sight wearing a fireman's hat, bulky sweater, oversized running shoes, and pajama bottoms. As we entered the back door of the house, I looked around. What a mess. The kitchen, back hallway, stairway, and my bedroom were all totally charred. My bedroom was located above the kitchen and had been completely destroyed. Mike's bedroom was relatively untouched. Surprisingly, my water-bed was still intact. The mattress was full of water but the firemen were pulling down sections of the ceiling onto it to put out spot fires in the attic insu-

lation (the next morning I found the mattress ruptured). I saw hangers where my two new suits—not yet paid for—used to hang. I found my car keys, but nothing else useful. This was going to be my easiest move. I found my alarm clock burned out at five minutes after midnight. That sent shivers up and down my spine. When I had originally run out onto the porch I had looked at my watch, and it said midnight. Without a doubt, I knew that God had saved my life and the life of my bother Mike. Looking back, this is the point in my life where I started my search for God. Several years later, I surrendered all and accepted Jesus Christ as my personal Saviour. Life has never been the same.

Back outside, my next door neighbor invited my brother and me to spend the night at his place. I didn't sleep. I just rested on his couch with a blanket over me until morning. With the sun just starting to rise, I knew that I couldn't delay my next task, no matter how much I dreaded it. I had to call my landlord and advise him that his house was not in the same condition as when he last saw it. I reluctantly dialed his number.

"Hello," my landlord Tony answered the phone.

"Tony, this is Steve Gallant," I said.

"Steve? Why are you calling me so early in the morning?"

"I've got some bad news about the house," I said.

I overheard his wife in the background curiously asking questions.

"What's happened?" Tony asked.

"There was a fire at the house." I told him. Tony repeated the news to his wife, who promptly started screaming that I had burned her house down.

"I give you an eviction notice and you burn down my house?" Tony yelled.

"No, Tony. The two events are unrelated. The fire was an accident. Mike left a pot of oil on the stove and it caught fire," I clarified.

Tony's wife continued screaming in the background.

"I have to go," Tony said. His wife was now totally hysterical.

"Tony, I'm sorry about the house," I said, but he hung up the phone without replying.

Next, I called my workplace to advise them that I needed the day off. They were very hesitant until I explained the reason and then they readily agreed. I asked to have my paycheck ready because of my urgent need for cash.

At the house I was able to salvage a ripped pair of jeans and a football sweater from the clothes dryer. The front hall closet provided me with a smelly jacket. That was it. I returned the sweater to my neighbor, thanked him, and promised to return the running shoes when I purchased some of my own. The pajama bottoms went in the back of my car. I got in, took a last look at what used to be my home, and drove away. It was the easiest move I have ever made.

I drove to work to get my paycheck. Luckily, the bank cashed the paycheck without having to show any identification. I didn't have any.

I was without the basics of life. When all you own in the world is either on your back or parked near by, you are forced to focus on the pure basics of survival: food, shelter, and clothing. Everything else in this world is a luxury. This concept is very difficult to grasp for a person raised in the western world.

I called my best friend, Don, and invited myself over to dinner. I ended up staying three years. I went and bought some clothes. The most frustrating process of trying to get a new social insurance number, a driver's license, and a birth certificate from the various government agencies. They kept asking me for identification, which I didn't have. To the government, I no longer existed. I was a non-person, a non-entity. I didn't even have an address to mail the items to. I was one of those people that you hear about the in news, a "John Doe of no fixed address."

The hardship didn't end with the fire. The insurance company who had insured the landlord for the structure of the house sued my brother and me for negligence. That's right, me! I was the guy who was asleep when the fire started. Worse yet, the insurance company turned out to be one of the three who had refused to insure my brother and me because they considered the place a "fire trap." Two years, eight months, and four days after the fire, I won a precedence setting case in Ontario court against the insurance company, which proved that a joint tenant could not be held libel for another tenant's negligence.

Mike, he was negligent and he lost the legal battle with the insurance company. After the judgment was passed, he immediately declared personal bankruptcy (I loaned him the money to do so), and never paid the insurance company a cent.

Epilogue

The first time that I gave my testimony at a Christian church, God revealed to me the following verse from the book of Isaiah:

> When thou passest through the waters, I will be with thee; and through the rivers, they shall not overflow thee: when thou walkest through the fire, thou shalt not be burned; neither shall the flames kindle upon thee.
>
> Isaiah 43:2